Know Your Numbers

Hands Down

Counting by Fives

by Michael Dahl   illustrated by Todd Ouren

Special thanks to our advisers for their expertise:

Stuart Farm, M.Ed., Mathematics Lecturer
University of North Dakota, Grand Forks

Susan Kesselring, M.A., Literacy Educator
Rosemount-Apple Valley-Eagan (Minnesota) School District

PICTURE WINDOW BOOKS
Minneapolis, Minnesota

Managing Editor: Catherine Neitge
Creative Director: Terri Foley
Art Director: Keith Griffin
Editor: Christianne Jones
Designer: Todd Ouren
Page production: Picture Window Books
The illustrations in this book were prepared digitally.

Picture Window Books
5115 Excelsior Boulevard
Suite 232
Minneapolis, MN 55416
877-845-8392
www.picturewindowbooks.com

Printed in the United States of America.

Library of Congress Cataloging-in-Publication Data
Dahl, Michael.
Hands down : counting by fives / written by Michael Dahl ;
illustrated by Todd Ouren.
p. cm. — (Know your numbers)
ISBN 1-4048-0948-1 (hardcover)
1. Counting—Juvenile literature. 2. Multiplication—Juvenile
literature. I. Ouren, Todd, ill. II. Title.

QA113.D334 2004
513.2'11—dc22   2004018431

Time for art class! Today we will be using our hands.

FIVE fingers make a happy handprint.

TEN fingers make a bright blue crab.

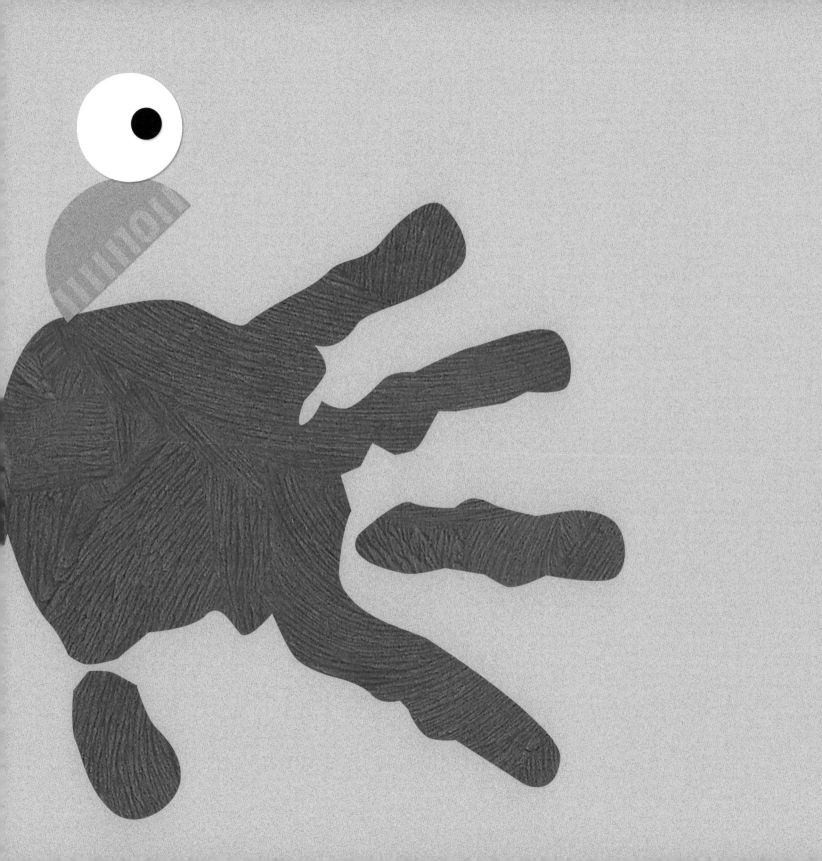

7

FIFTEEN fingers make lovely leaves on an old oak tree.

5 10 15

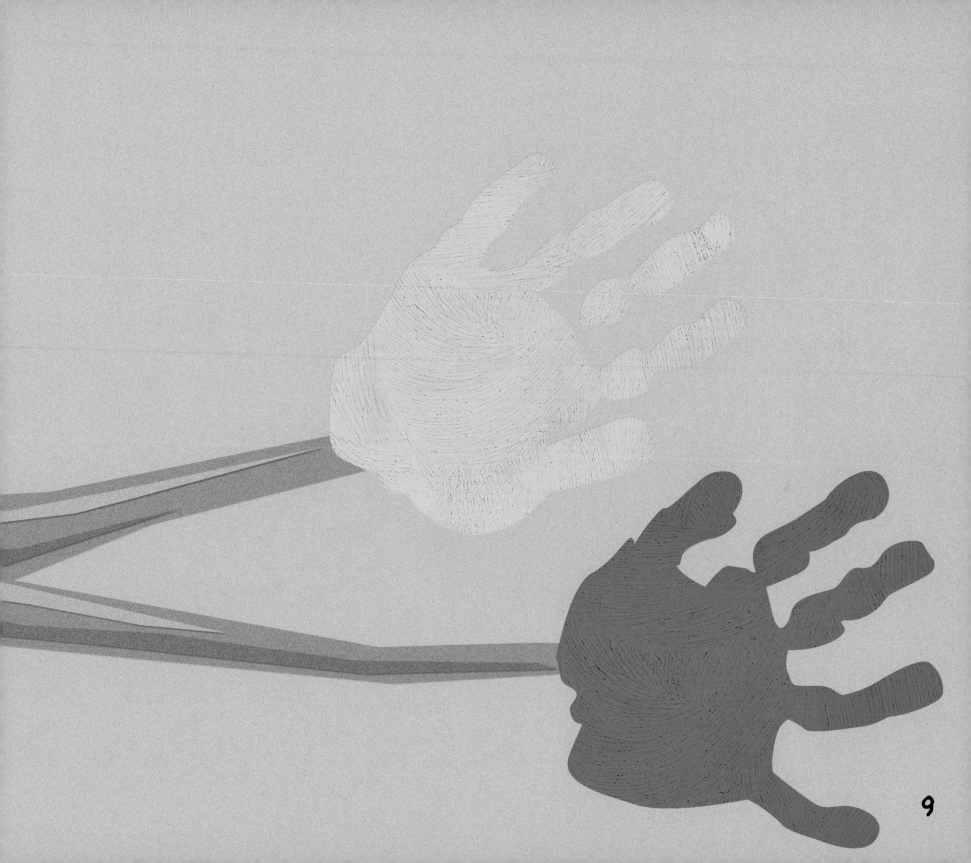

9

TWENTY fingers make beautiful butterflies.

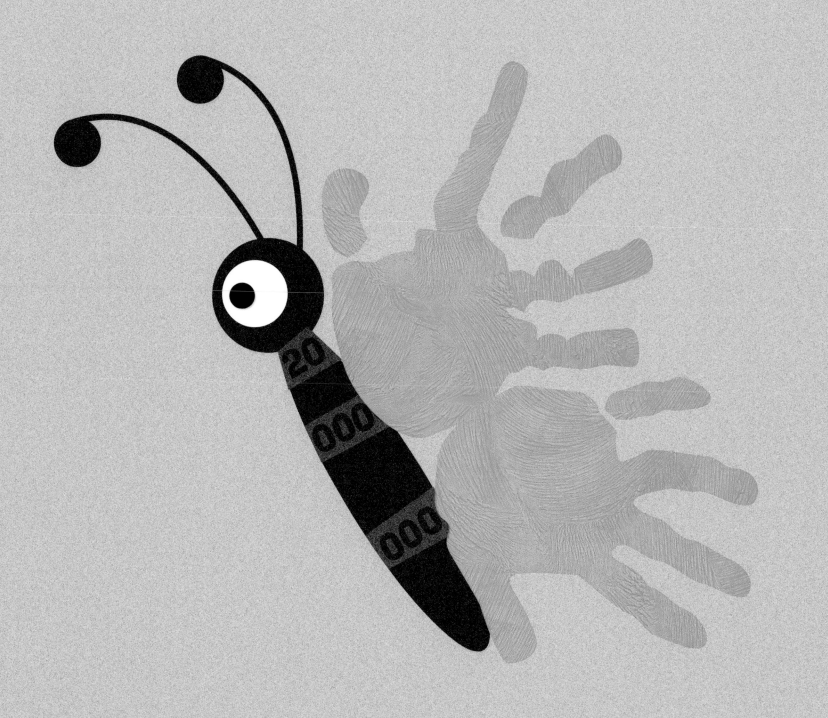

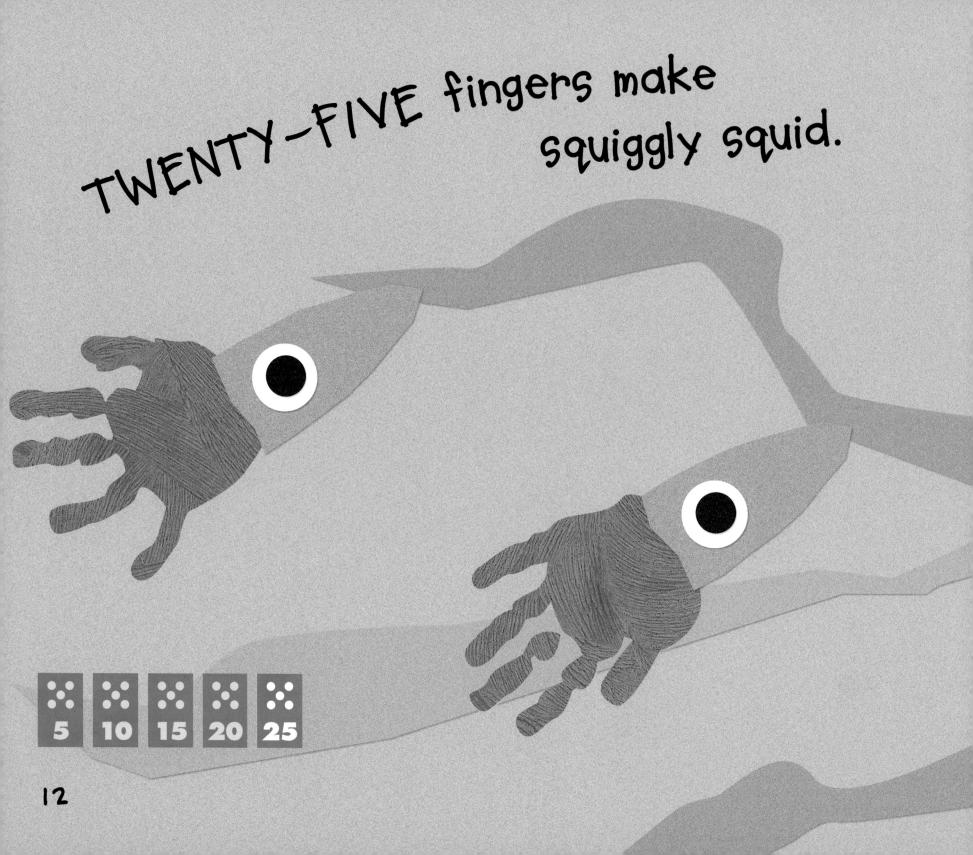

TWENTY-FIVE fingers make squiggly squid.

5 10 15 20 25

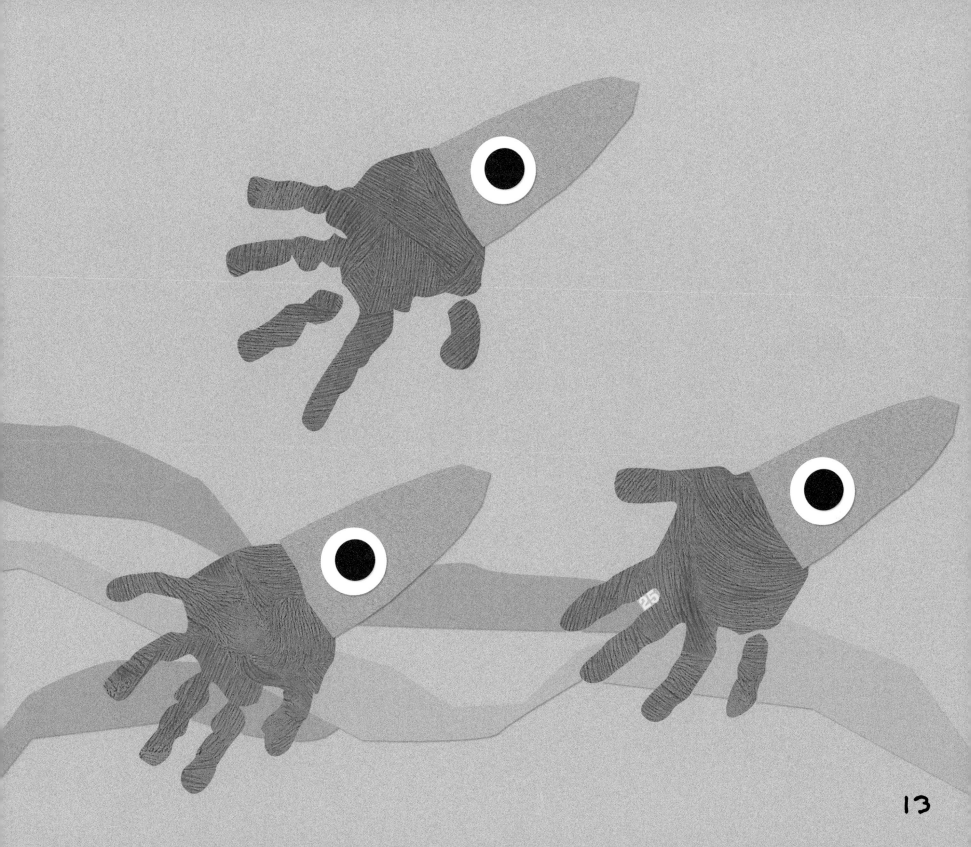

13

THIRTY fingers make kissing turkeys.

5 10 15 20 25 30

14

15

THIRTY-FIVE fingers make gloomy ghosts.

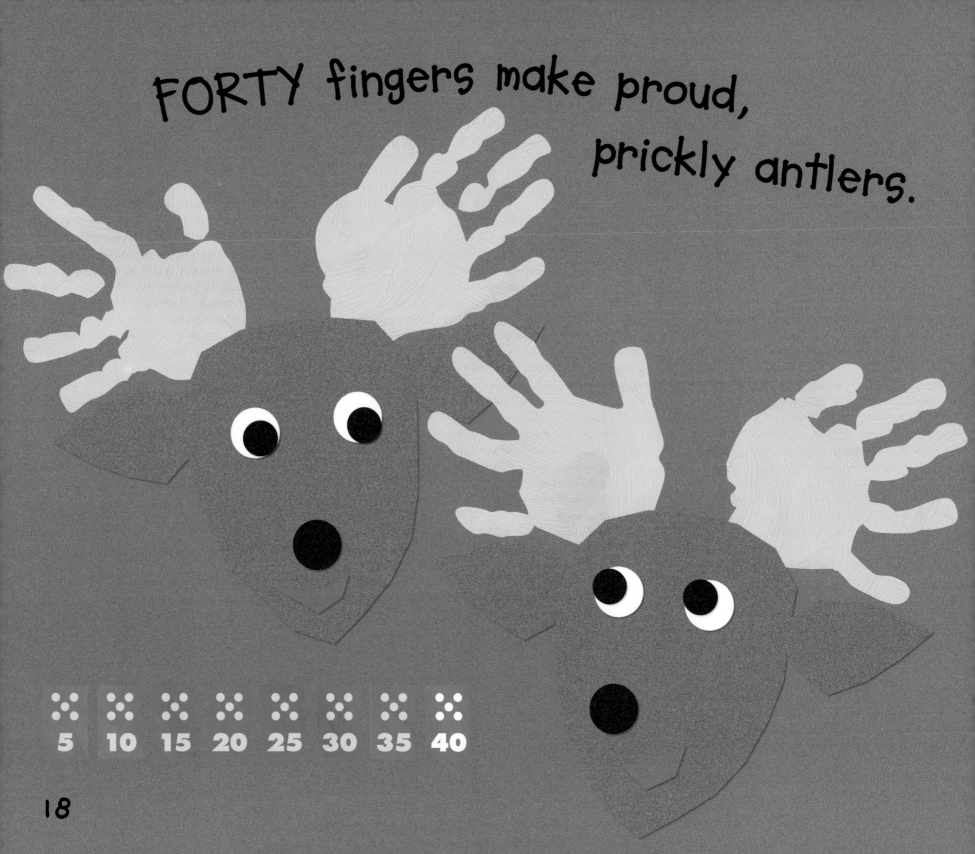

FORTY fingers make proud, prickly antlers.

5 10 15 20 25 30 35 40

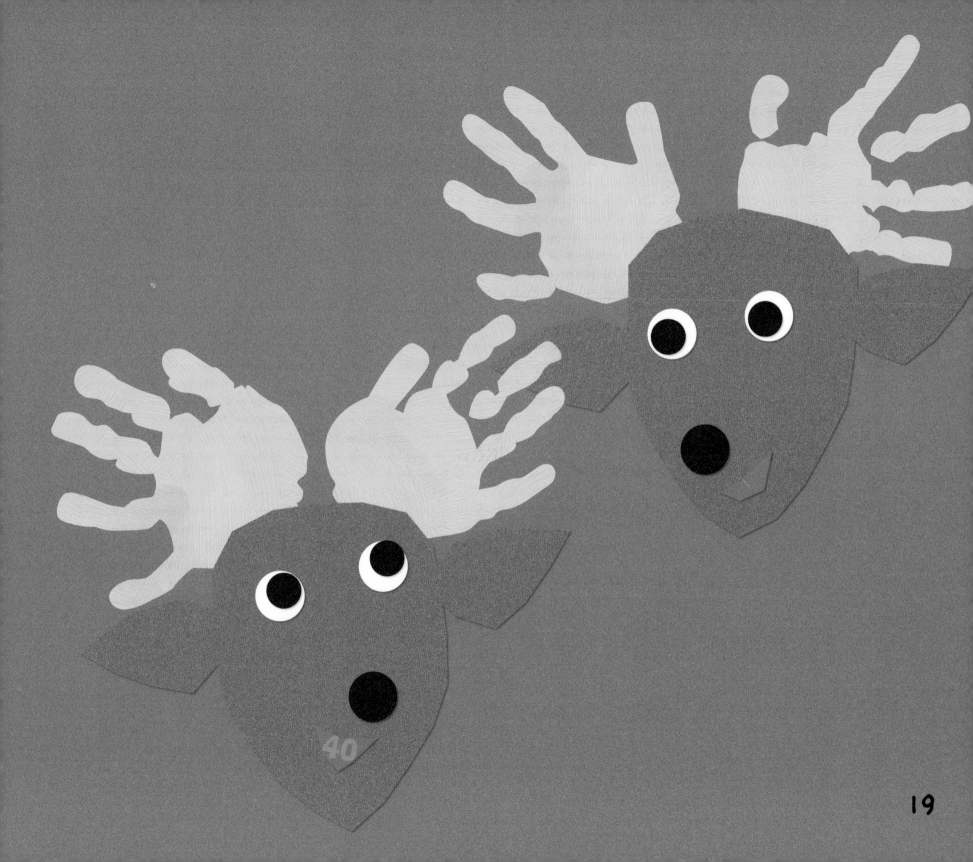

19

FORTY-FIVE fingers make a spectacular spring garden.

5 10 15 20 25 30 35 40 45

21

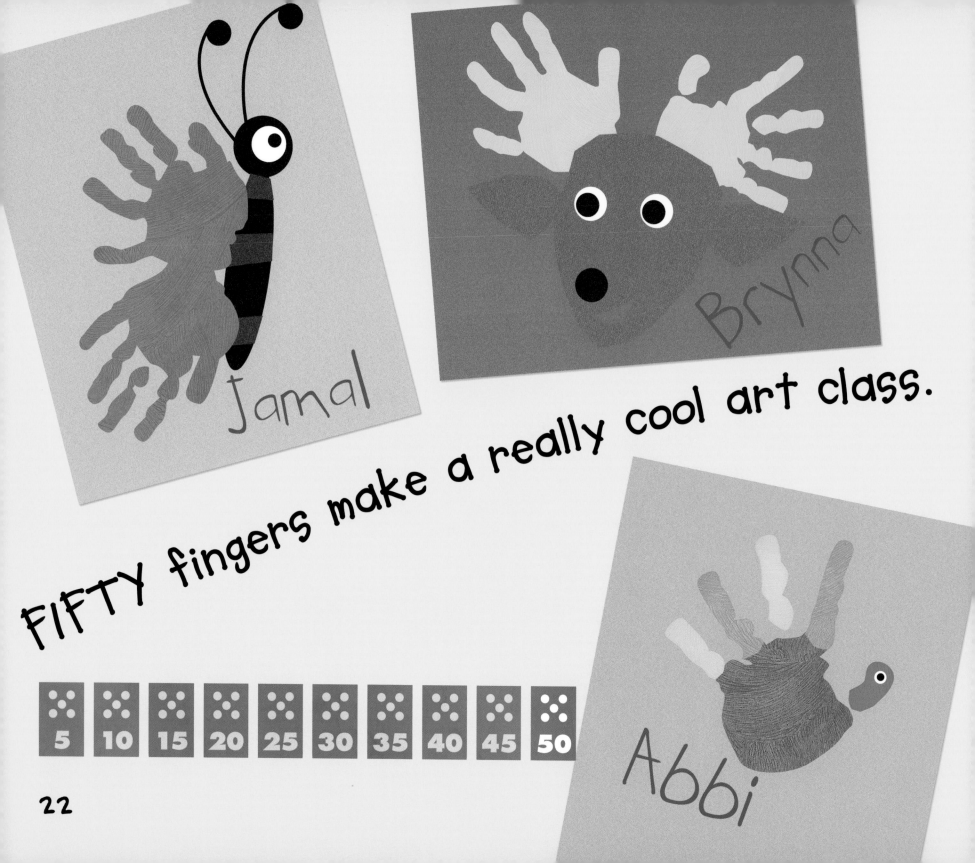

Jamal

Brynna

FIFTY fingers make a really cool art class.

| 5 | 10 | 15 | 20 | 25 | 30 | 35 | 40 | 45 | 50 |

Abbi

22

Connor

Charlie

Matt

Aisha

23

Fun Facts

Blue crabs bury themselves in soft mud or sand during cold, winter months. They stop eating until it gets warm again.

Butterflies taste their food with their feet.

Some squid have eyes that are as big as soccer balls.

Male turkeys are called toms, and female turkeys are called hens. Only toms gobble.

Elk and deer shed their antlers each year. In the spring, the animals grow new antlers.

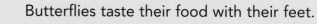
Oak trees get struck by lightning more than any other type of tree.

On the Web

FactHound offers a safe, fun way to find Web sites related to this book. All of the sites on FactHound have been researched by our staff. *www.facthound.com*

1. Visit the FactHound home page.
2. Enter a search word related to this book, or type in this special code: 1404809481
3. Click on the FETCH IT button.

Your trusty FactHound will fetch the best Web sites for you!

24

Find the Numbers

Now you have finished reading the story, but a surprise still awaits you. Hidden in each picture is a multiple of 5 from 5 to 50. Can you find them all?

5–near the top of the bowl

10–under the right eye of the blue crab

15–in the large knothole

20–on the neck of the orange butterfly

25–between the tentacles of the fifth squid

30–on the heads of the turkeys on the top right

35–on the body of the bottom bat

40–in the mouth of the third reindeer

45–on the blue flower on the right

50–on the squid's middle tentacle

Look for all of the books in the Know Your Numbers series: